RIP ROARING ANIMAL JOKES

Animal Cracker Uppers

RICHARD LEDERER & JIM ERTNER

International Punsters of the Year

ILLUSTRATIONS BY JIM MCLEAN

Marion Street Press

Portland, Oregon

To Ted Croll, who cares for and who cares so much about children. —*Richard Lederer*

To my daughter Gail and grandson Bryce: two generations that have listened to my jokes. —*Jim Ertner*

Published by Marion Street Press
4207 SE Woodstock Blvd # 168
Portland, OR 97206-6267
USA
http://www.marionstreetpress.com/
Orders and review copies: (800) 888-4741
Copyright © 2012 by Richard Lederer and Jim Ertner
Illustrations copyright © 2012 by Jim McLean
All rights reserved.
Printed in the United States of America
ISBN 978-1-936863-16-7

Library of Congress Cataloging-in-Publication Data Pending

CONTENTS

PART 1
A Dictionary of Animal Jokes

PART 2
Even More Animal Jokes

INTRODUCTION

Animals
       scamper and scramble
              hop and slither,
                     and burrow and dig
through our everyday lives.

Animals live in our language:
       "hungry as a horse (or bear),"
              "quiet as a mouse,"
                     "proud as a peacock,"
                            "nervous as a cat,"
                                   and "snug as a bug in a rug."

Animals become symbols of athletic excellence:
       the Chicago Bulls,
              the Charlotte Bobcats,
                     the Seattle Seahawks,
                            the Pittsburgh Penguins,
                                   and the Tampa Bay Rays.
And everybody loves animal jokes:
    Cheetah jokes never prosper, but as King of the Jungle,
    lion jokes rule.
    Mountain goat jokes rock.
    Oyster jokes contain pearls of wisdom.
    And kangaroo jokes are the best by leaps and bounds.

Here are more than 500 animal jokes that are guaranteed
to make you
        bellow,
            bray,
                hee-haw,
                    and screech
with lots of laughter.

PART 1
A DICTIONARY
OF ANIMAL JOKES

Alligator

Did you hear about the new TV show about alligators?

It was so popular that the TV station was swamped with calls.

What do you call a hot-headed crocodile that is quick to start a fight?

An insta-gator.

Amoeba

Did you hear about the amoeba state prison?

It's so small that it has only one cell.

Animals (in general)

Where do chickens, sheep, cows, goats, and horses go to get their prescriptions filled?

Old MacDonald's Farm-acy.

The Animal Fair

I went to the animal fair.
The birds and the beasts were there.
The big baboon, by the light of the moon,
Was combing his auburn hair.

You should have seen the monk.
He climbed up the elephant's trunk.

The elephant sneezed and fell to his knees,
And that was the end of the monk.

The animal fair, the animal fair,
We had such fun when we were there.
There never was a fair to compare
With that rollicking, frolicking animal fair.

Did you hear about the man who broke into an animal store?

He was charged with petty theft.

Ant

How many relatives went on the picnic?

Three uncles and 100,000 ants.

I've seen an antelope, but I've never seen an ant elope.

What do insects take when they're ill?

Ant-ibiotics.

What do you call someone who buys and sells old bugs?
An ant-ique dealer.

A first-time airplane passenger looked out the window and marveled to his companion, "Look at those tiny people down there. They look like ants."

"They are ants," came the reply. "We haven't taken off yet."

Ape

What do you call crazy gorillas?
Ape nut flakes.

As one monkey said to the other, "Why did I go ape over that baboon?"

When do monkeys fall from the sky?
During Ape-ril showers.

Baboon

What kind of monkey is always exploding?
A baBOOM.

Bat

What did the mother bat say to the father bat?
"We'll soon hear the batter of little feet around the cave."

Why was night baseball started?
Because bats like to sleep in the daytime.

Beagle

What does Snoopy eat for breakfast?

Beagle and cream cheese.

What do you call a dog who is a lawyer?

A legal beagle.

Bear

Did you hear about the singers in Yellowstone National Park?

They're bear-itones.

A little girl told her parents that her Sunday school class sang a song about a bear named Gladly who wore glasses. The parents were puzzled and asked their daughter to sing the song for them. So the child sang, "Gladly, the Cross-Eyed Bear."

What does a grizzly call honey and a warm cave?

The bear necessities of life.

What is the sign of a successful bear businessman?

One who claws his way to the top.

Beaver

How should you feel in the presence of a beaver ghost?

Be afraid. Beaver-y afraid.

Bee

Why is it easier to spell "bees" than "ants"?

Because it's spelled with more "e"'s.

Why do bees work so hard?

They like to keep buzzy.

Where do space bees go after they get married?

On a honeymoon.

Why do bees have sticky hair?

Because they always use honey combs.

What's the favorite song in a hive?

"Bee it ever so humble, there's no place like comb."

What is black and yellow and goes "zzub, zzub"?

A bee flying backwards.

A man came running to the doctor shouting and screaming in pain. "Please, doctor, you've got to help me. I've been stung by a bee!"

"Don't worry," said the doctor. "I'll put some cream on it."

"You will never find that bee. It must be miles away by now."

"No, you don't understand!" answered the doctor. "I'll put some cream on the place you were stung."

"Oh! It happened in the garden behind my house."

"No, no, no!" explained the doctor, getting frustrated. "I mean on the part of your body the bee stung you."

"On my finger!" screamed the man in pain. "The bee stung me on my finger, and it really hurts!"

"Which one?" the doctor asked.

"How am I supposed to know? All bees look the same to me!"

Bird

Did you hear about the bird that flew into a can of varnish and drowned?

It was a sad way to die, but the bird sure had a beautiful finish.

Did you hear about the woman who eats like a bird?

A peck at a time.

What birds are always unhappy?

Bluebirds.

What do you call a bird that looks like all the other birds in his group?

A chirp off the old flock.

Bloodhound

Did you hear about the neurotic bloodhound?

He thought that people were following him.

Boa

What do you get if you cross some pasta with a boa?

Spaghetti that winds itself around a fork.

Boxer

What breed of dog most often gets into fights?

Boxers.

A psychiatrist suggested that a Boxer with insomnia try counting sheep.

"I've already tried that," replied the Boxer. "And every time, just before I reach 10, I stand up."

Buffalo

What does the buffalo on old nickels stand for?
Because there's no room for him to sit down.

Bug

What is a bug's favorite kissing game?
Spin the beetle.

What is a bug's favorite questioning device?
A fly detector.

What is a bug's favorite fall drink?
Apple spider.

Did you hear the one about the man who was accidentally bitten by the star flea in a flea circus?
The doctor ordered him to recuperate for a week. During his time off, he visited Hollywood and won a small part in a film. He thus was the first person to become an actor because he was bitten by an acting bug.

Burro

How do donkeys search for buried treasure?
They burro down after it.

Butterfly

What do nuts chase after with little nets?
Peanut butterflies.

Camel

What is the favorite Christmas carol in the Arabian desert?

"Oh Camel Ye Faithful."

Canary

What do you call a victorious boxing canary?

A featherweight champion.

Where do canaries go when they have feet trouble?

To the chirpodist.

Carp

What game do young fish enjoy playing?
Carps and robbers.

Cat

Did you hear about the cat who was walking along the beach on Christmas Eve?
He had sandy claws.

What do cats call other cats' purrs?
Meow-sic to their ears.

What do cats read for current events?
The daily mewspaper.

Where did the kittens go on their class trip?
To a mew-see-'em.

Why is a cat drinking milk like a track star?
Because they both enjoy taking a few laps.

What did the cat say when its tail got caught in a lawn mower?
"It won't be long now."

Caterpillar

What pillar is never used to hold up a building?
A caterpillar.

Cattle

Where do cows go for entertainment?
To the moovies and to amoosment parks.

What is the Golden Rule for cows?

"Do unto udders as you would have udders do unto you."

Did you hear about the bowlegged cowboy?

He couldn't keep his calves together.

Why did the chef watch the lazy cow?

He wanted to see the meat loaf.

Did you hear about the matador who became a baseball player?

She could always be found in the bull pen.

How did the bullfight end?

It was a toss up.

Centipede

What is a centipede's favorite toy?

Leg-os.

What has 100 feet and 98 shoes?

A centipede trying on a new pair of loafers.

Teacher: "Why are you late to school?"

Centipede student: "My mother was playing 'This little piggy went to market' with me."

Did you hear about the centipede that came home late one night and was afraid of waking his wife?

He wanted to sneak upstairs, but he spent the whole night taking off his shoes.

Did you hear about the new book titled *Insects with Many Legs*?

It's by Millie Pede.

Chameleon

Did you hear about Benedict Arnold's pet chameleon?
It turned its coat from Colonial blue to British red.

Chicken

Patient: "Doctor, doctor! My wife thinks she's been a chicken for the past year."
Doctor: "Why didn't you bring her to see me sooner?"
Patient: "We needed the eggs."

Why did the chicken run away from home?
It was tired of being cooped up.

Why was Superman able to catch the runaway chicken?
Because Superman is faster than a speeding pullet.

What do baby chickens like to read?
Peeple Magazine.

Chimpanzee

What did the chimpanzee say when his sister had a baby?
"Well, I'll be a monkey's uncle."

What language do chimpanzees speak?
Chimpanese.

Clam

What do you call a breeding ground for shellfish?
Clam and eggs.

Cockroach

As one insect said to another, "Why haven't you written? After all, I roach you a letter."

Cod

What did the fisherman say to the magician?
"Go ahead. Pick a cod. Any cod."

Collie

Did you hear about the dog that ate a cantaloupe?
She felt rather melon collie.

Crab

Did you hear about the crab who played the violin?
He was a fiddler on the reef.

A crab isn't the only one to have a crab for a mate.

Crane

What bird flies over 74 miles per hour?
A hurricrane.

Cricket

What is the grasshopper's favorite sport?
Cricket.

What is the Jiminy Cricket computer virus?
It changes your zip file into a zip-a-dee doo-dah file.

Crocodile

Patient: "Doctor, doctor! I keep seeing pink-striped crocodiles."

Doctor: "Have you seen a psychiatrist?"

Patient: "No, only pink-striped crocodiles."

Crow

Why did the baby blackbird cry?
Because it had crowing pains.

A crow never complains without caws.

Dachshund

What is taller sitting down than standing up?
A dachshund.

Why is the dachshund a good family dog?
Because all the members of the family can pet it at the same time.

Deer

Did you hear about the deer that was almost shot by an archer?

It had an arrow escape.

One husband to another: "I don't think my wife loves me anymore. She bought me a deerskin coat for when I go hunting."

Dinosaur

Did you hear about the prehistoric animal that exercised too much?

It was a dino-sore.

Did you hear about the prehistoric animal that slept noisily?

It was a dino-snore.

How would you move a 1,000-ton dinosaur?

With dino-mite.

What do you call a scared dinosaur?

A nervous rex.

What do you get when dinosaurs crash their cars?

Tyrannosaurus wrecks.

Doe

What happened when two deer met at a square dance?

Doe-see-doe.

Dog

I've got some good news and some bad news. The good news is that my girlfriend invited me for dinner and asked me to pick up some dog food on the way over. The bad news is that she doesn't have a dog.

A dog owner was looking for a place to board his pet while he went on vacation. He found one kennel that offered air conditioning, gourmet food, and lots of affection. He was so impressed that he sent his dog on vacation and HE stayed at the kennel.

What did the veterinarian have on his vanity license plate?
K-9.

What's the opposite of a cool cat?
A hot dog.

What do you call a cold canine?
A chili dog.

Why does a dog get so hot in the summer?
Because he wears a coat and pants.

Dolphin

How does a group of dolphins make a decision?
Flipper coin.

Dragon

How did the dragon observe the Sabbath?
He only preyed on weak knights.

Why did the mother dragon complain about her twins?
She couldn't extinguish them apart.

Duck

Why are duck actors so arrogant?

> *Because they always want top billing.*

Why do ducks often look so sad?

> *Because when they preen their feathers, they get down in the mouth.*

Did you hear about the two ducks in a race?

> *It resulted in the thrill of victory and the agony of webbed feet.*

A visitor on horseback came to a stream and asked a young boy if the water was deep. "No," replied the lad. Thus, the rider started to cross the stream, but soon found himself submerged. Upon reaching the other side, the traveler shouted at the boy, "I thought you said it wasn't deep!"

"It isn't," the boy replied. "It only comes up to the middle of ducks."

Eagle

What bird never goes to a barber?

A bald eagle

Two guys were walking along the beach when one pointed overhead and exclaimed, "Look at the eagle!"

The other guy replied, "That doesn't look like an eagle."

"That's not surprising," added the former, "since eagles are masters of de skies."

Eel

How do you catch an electric eel?
With a lightning rod.

A speedy young swimmer named Block
Was the fastest away from the dock.
He broke records galore
Till they found that he wore
An electric eel stuffed in his jock.

Elephant

Why did the baby elephant put its teeth under its pillow?
For the tusk fairy.

What does an elephant use to wash his tusks?
Ivory Soap.

How do you make an elephant fly?
First, you get a huge zipper . . . .

Did you hear about the guy who gave up hunting elephants?
The decoys were too heavy.

What do you give a seasick elephant?
Plenty of room.

Elk

What did the deer do about his indigestion?
He took some elk-a-seltzer.

Ewe

I'd buy a sculpture of a female sheep. Wooden ewe?

Finch

How can a dozen birds look like a foot?
> *When they're 12 finches.*

Firefly

What did one firefly say to another?
> *"What time are you going out tonight?"*

What did the firefly say after it flew into a screen door?
> *"Delighted, no end."*

Fish

What did one bass say to another?
"Keep your big mouth shut, and you won't get caught!"

What did the Cinderella fish wear to the ball?
Glass flippers.

Why are fish poor tennis players?
They don't like to play too close to the net.

Why did the optometrist go ice fishing?
She had perfect ice site.

What happened to the boat that sank in the sea full of piranha fish?
It came back with a skeleton crew.

What part of a fish is like the end of this section?
The fin-ish.

Flamingo

Did you hear about the family of flamingos?
They decorated their front lawn with plastic humans.

Flea

How do you start a flea race?
By shouting, "One, two, flea, go!"

How do fleas travel?
They itch-hike.

What is the highest rank in the insect navy?
Flea-t admiral.

Why did the flea live on the dog's chin?
He wanted a woof over his head.

Some say that fleas are black,
But I know that is not so,
'Cause Mary had a little lamb
With fleas as white as snow.

Fly

Have you ever seen a horse fly?

Then there was the guy who's not a very good artist, but he sure draws flies.

Why will the computer never replace the newspaper?
You can't swat flies and line the bottom of a birdcage with a computer.

As one frog said to another as they sat on a lily pad, "Time's fun when you're having flies."

Foal

Why did the police investigate the young horse's accident?
They suspected foal play.

Fowl

Where do chickens hold their formal dance?
At the fowl ball.

Frog

How many frogs does it take to change a light bulb?
Just one—if he hops to it.

Patient: "Doctor, doctor! I keep seeing frogs in front of my eyes."
Doctor: "Don't worry, it's only a hoptical illusion."

Why couldn't the python talk?
Because it had a frog in its throat.

What do you call a frog with a cast on each of its back legs?
Unhoppy.

What do frogs wear for a night out on the town?
Jumpsuits.

A frog named Kermit Jagger went to a bank for a second mortgage on his lily pad. He asked the mortgage officer, a Miss Patricia Whack, if he could borrow a certain sum of money. When she asked him for some collateral, the frog gave her a small trinket. She then took the object into the manager's office, explained the whole story, and concluded by saying, "I'd love to let him borrow the money, but I don't know what this trinket is."

The manager replied, "It's a knickknack, Patty Whack. Give the frog a loan. His old man's a Rolling Stone."

Gander

What's the motto of Kenya, Africa?
"What's good for the goose is good for Uganda."
(Kenya believe that?)

Giraffe

Did you hear about the nearsighted basketball player?
He asked a giraffe out on a date.

Why is the giraffe the smartest animal in the jungle?
It has a high level of intelligence.

Why did the lion ask a giraffe to marry him?

Two other lions put him up to it.

Did you hear about the congestion at the zoo?

There was a giraffic jam.

Does a giraffe develop a head cold after it gets its feet wet?

Yes, but not until a week later.

Gnat

What do you get if you cross an amnesiac and an insect?

A forget-me-gnat.

Gnu

What did Santa Claus tell his reindeer?

"If you don't stop misbehaving, I may get a gnu sleigh."

Or, as one antelope said to another on January 1, "Happy Gnu Year!"

Why did the ant elope?

Nobody gnu.

Goat

Goats have bad manners. They are always butting in.

Who babysits for the kids?

A nanny goat.

Did you hear about the rabbit that was eaten by a goat?

It became a hare in the butter.

Goldfish

Mom: "Have you given the goldfish fresh water today?"

Son: "They haven't finished drinking what I gave them yesterday."

Goose

I wanted to buy some goose feathers, but I couldn't afford the down payment.

Did you hear about the two geese that had a mid-air collision?

Fortunately, all they got were goose bumps.

Gorilla

What did the gorilla call his wife?

His prime-mate.

Where does an 800-pound gorilla sit?

Anywhere she wants to.

A man bought a giant gorilla and was told that all he had to do was feed his gorilla three bananas three times a day. But he was never ever, ever to touch its fur.

The next day the man came and gave the gorilla a banana and looked at it for a while thinking, "Why can't I touch its fur?" So he did.

The gorilla immediately went ape and started to jump up and down, beating its chest. Then it turned and began running toward the man, who, of course, was scared out of his mind. There was no escape. As the gorilla neared him, the man began to feel faint.

The giant beast came face to face with the man, raised its mighty hand, and bellowed, "Tag! You're it!"

Grasshopper

While vacationing in Australia, a typical Texan was bragging about his big state, when a kangaroo hopped by. The Texan was visibly impressed and drawled, "I must admit that your grasshoppers are bigger than ours."

Greyhound

Did you hear about the funny-looking greyhound dog that had a bus painted on its side?

Groundhog

Did you hear about the student who saw her shadow on Groundhog Day and predicted six more weeks of detention?

Hamster

Did you hear about the boy who ended up with 10 hamsters?

His female hamster's "sister" turned out to be a himster.

Hare

Breeding rabbits is a hare-raising experience.

What is a rabbit's favorite exercise?
  Hareobics.

As the magician said when she couldn't find the rabbit she had put in her hat, "Hare today, gone tomorrow."

I was walking through the forest one fine day in January and heard an unusual barking sound. I carefully crept toward the sound, and suddenly spied an unusual looking rabbit barking like a dog. But when I called the biology department at the university to report my new discovery, they hung up on me. I guess they just weren't interested in my Yappy New Hare.

Hawk

What bird has a funny-looking haircut?
  A Mohawk.

Heifer

What is a bull's favorite love song?
  "If heifer I should lose you."

Hen

Did you hear about the hen that received amorous advances from a rooster?
  She egged him on.

Did you hear about the hen who misbehaved in school?
  She was eggspelled.

What do you get if you cross a hen and some gunpowder?

An eggsplosion.

The codfish lays 10,000 eggs,
The lonely hen lays one.
The codfish never cackles
To tell you what she's done.
And so we scorn the codfish,
While the humble hen we prize,
Which only goes to show you
That it pays to advertise.

Herring

Did you hear about the partially deaf fish?

She was hard of herring.

Hippopotamus

There once was a jolly fat hippo
Who jumped in the sea for a dippo.
It would have been wise
Had he opened his eyes,
But he didn't and flattened a ship, oh!

Hog

There once was a lazy, green frog
Who rode on the back of a dog.
But the dog wasn't big,
So he moved to a pig.
You could say that he's going whole hog.

Why are hogs like trees?
They root for a living.

Horse

Did you hear about the dejected horse?
He had a long face and told a tale of whoa.

How do you make a slow horse fast?
Don't feed it anything.

When does a horse eat the most?
When it has a little bit in its mouth.

She was only a stableman's daughter, but all the horsemen knew 'er.

Why did the superstitious jockey compete at only one racetrack?
He had a one-track mind.

What did the horse lying on the ground say to the doctor?
"I've fallen and I can't giddyup!"

Did you hear about the horse that was so slow during a race that the jockey kept a diary of the trip?

Why is a leaking faucet like a racehorse?
Because it's off and running.

Hyena

Did you hear about the unsuccessful stand-up comic who couldn't even make a hyena laugh?

Insect

What happened when insects attacked a potato crop?
The farmer kept his eyes peeled.

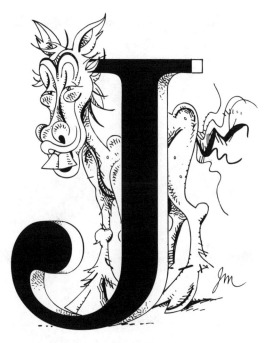

Jackass

Speaker (to heckler): "Please be quiet, sir. I have only 30 minutes to make a jackass of myself. You have a whole lifetime."

Kangaroo

Why did the kangaroo throw her daughter out of the pouch?
For eating crackers in bed.

Why did the baby kangaroo refuse to hop into a neighbor's pouch?
Because it wasn't his bag.

Why do politicians like kangaroos to make campaign contributions?
Because they have deep pockets.

What do you call a baby kangaroo that can't jump yet?
An offspring.

Kid

Did you hear about the couple that is perfectly matched?

He's a funny old goat, and she's a great kidder.

Kitten

Did you hear about the two punsters who told a lot of jokes about kittens?

"We won't tell any more," they said. "And we're not kitten about that either."

Kiwi

A kiwi is an unflappable bird.

Lemming

What advice did the mother lemming give to her son?

"Just because Johnny is jumping off a cliff doesn't mean you have to."

Leopard

What happened to the leopard that took a bath three times a day?

After a week, he was spotless.

How can a leopard change his spots?

By moving.

Lion

Did you hear about the best-selling jungle book entitled *Never Make a Lioness Angry?*
> *It's by Sheila Tack.*

Did you hear about the fellow who mowed his lawn while whirling a whip?
> *He was the dandelion tamer.*

What's the best way to talk to a lion?
> *Long distance.*

What is a lion's favorite food?
> *Baked beings.*

How does a lion greet the other animals in the field?
> *"Pleased to eat you."*

What do lions sing at Christmas?
> *Jungle Bells, Jungle Bells.*

A famous trumpeter was on safari in the jungles of Africa and spent his evenings serenading the wild animals. The way he was able to tame the hungry beasts with his beautiful tones was uncanny. One evening, however, a lone lion leaped out of the brush and devoured the horn player. The other animals severely criticized him and asked how he could destroy the creator of such melodious music.

The killer lion turned his head, held a paw to his ear, and said, "You'll have to shout. I'm hard of hearing."

Lizard

What has a long tongue and walks on yellow brick roads?

The Lizard of Oz.

Who rules the royal reptile kingdom?

Queen Elizardbeth.

Llama

What do South American animals use to help them wake up?

A llama clock.

Lobster

A lobster is one who can aim the ball over his opponent's head on a tennis court.

Locust

What insect cursed in a quiet voice?

A locust.

Lox

Workers in a deli were permitted to eat anything during their scheduled spare time except smoked salmon. These, thus, became the world's first anti-lox breaks.

Mole

Why did the mole build a new house?
He was fed up with the hole thing.

Monkey

Why did the chimpanzee like potato chips?
She was a chipmonkey.

What is a monkey's favorite fruit-flavored drink?
Oranga-Tang.

Moose

How can you distinguish a male elk from a fe
By his moosetache.

Moth

Two actresses were comparing their wardrobes. One said, "I choose my own clothes."

The other replied, "A moth chews mine."

Mouse

A mouse that was mad about cheese
Developed a terrible sneeze.
His problem was this:
The holes in the Swiss
Admitted too much of a breeze.

What famous mouse lived in ancient Rome?

Julius Cheeser.

Why is an old loaf of bread like a mouse dashing into its hole?

Because you can see it's stale.

One mouse to another in a laboratory cage: "I've got that scientist trained. Whenever I press this lever, he gives me food."

What do cats like on their hot dogs?

Catsup and mousetard.

What has gray skin, four legs, and a trunk?

No, not an elephant—but a mouse on vacation.

Mynah

What birds wear helmets down in the pits?

Coal mynahs.

Newt

What is a salamander's favorite treat?
Fig Newt-ons.

Nightingale

What weather do nightingales hate the most?
Spending a night in gales.

Ocelot

Did you hear about the ocelot that is deeply in debt?
It really owes a lot.

Octopus

An octopus has two pairs of forearms.

What kind of cat likes water?
An octopuss.

Orca

Where do killer whales play their musical instruments?
In the orca-stra.

Ostrich

An ostrich arrived late to a beach party at which all the other guests had their heads buried in the sand. The latecomer looked around and then announced, "Where is everybody?"

Otter

Why did the web-footed animal cross the road?
To get to the otter side.

Owl

Did you hear about the book on detective owls?
It's a whooo-done-it.

What does an owl in the daytime have in common with the 16th president of the United States?
They're both A-blinkin'.

Did you hear about the indifferent owl?
He just doesn't give a hoot.

Ox

Did you hear about the two oxen that bumped into each other?
It was just an oxident.

Oyster

What is chocolate and lies on the bottom of the ocean?

An oyster egg.

As the Australian fisherman shouted when a woman fell off the pier, "'Oyster up!'"

According to experts, the oyster
In its shell, or crustacean cloister,
May frequently be
Either he or a she
Or both, if it should be its choice ter.

Panda

What do you call chaos among pandas?

Pandamonium.

Parrot

A parrot never said a word until its seventh birthday. Finally, during a meal it blurted out, "This piece of fruit is stale!"

The parrot's owner exclaimed, "You can talk! Why haven't you spoken before?"

The parrot replied, "Well, so far everything's been okay."

After a woman purchased a parrot at an auction, she asked the auctioneer, "Are you sure this parrot talks? I've bid an awful lot of money on it."

The man replied, "I'm quite sure. After all, the parrot was bidding against you."

What's orange and sounds like a parrot?
A carrot.

Peacock

A peacock is a chicken in bloom.

Why is the figure "9" like a peacock?
Because it's nothing without its tail.

Pelican

Why did the pelican put a leg in his beak when he ate in a restaurant?
He wanted to foot the bill.

Penguin

Did you hear about the formal dance at the zoo?
The penguins wore tuxedoes, and the monkeys wore tails.

Why did the penguins dress in T-shirts and shorts the next day?
It was casual Friday.

How does a penguin make pancakes?
With its flippers.

Pheasant

A flea once lived on a pheasant
Who was royally vain and unpleasant,
Till the flea, on a whim,
Bit the "h" out of him;
And now he is only a peasant.

Pig

Did you hear about the pigs' dinner?
It was a real swill meal.

How does a pig with laryngitis feel?
Disgruntled.

Did you hear about the truck that carried a dozen and a half pigs?
It was an 18-squealer.

Show us a sausage factory that covers an entire acre, and we'll show you a lot of baloney.

Pigeon

What kind of bird is the least trustworthy?
A stool pigeon.

Platypus

What animal might you serve dinner on?
A platterpus.

Polar Bear

Where do white bears vote?
At the North Poll.

Polliwog

A princess who lived near a bog
Met a prince in the form of a frog.
Now she and her prince
Are the parents of quints:
Four girls and one polliwog.

Poodle

Some dogs are called miniature poodles because the miniature back is turned they make a poodle.

Porcupine

What do porcupines have that no other animal has?
Baby porcupines.

In a school debate between a porcupine and a wolf, the porcupine won on points.

What's worse than a rhinoceros on water skis?
A porcupine on a rubber raft.

What is a porcupine's favorite food?
Prickled onions.

Porpoise

A Boy Scout troop was on a camping trip near an ocean beach. Every evening friendly dolphins swam toward shore for their meal. The scout leader called everyone to dinner by shouting, "It's chow time, for all in tents and porpoises."

Puppy

What did the minister say when he saw the damage to his favorite flowers done by his young dog?
"They're the ones my pup runneth over."

Quail

What did the game birds sing at the family reunion?
"Quail, quail, the gang's all here."

Rabbit

What do you call a rabbit who has never left the house?
An ingrown hare.

> *The habits of rabbits*
> *Are such, it's agreed,*
> *That dozens of cousins*
> *Are common indeed.*

What happens when a rabbit hole becomes overheated?
You get a hot cross bunny.

Ram

What is a sheep's favorite movie character?
Rambo.

Rat

The problem with rat races is that, even if you win, you're still a rat.

Rattlesnake

How do you make a baby or a snake cry?
Take away its rattle.

Reindeer

Wife: "How is a cloud like Santa Claus?"
Husband: "It holds rain, dear."

Rhinoceros

A rhino never blows its own horn.

Robin

Why did Batman go to the pet store?
To buy a Robin.

Rooster

Husband: "Remember, I rule the roost here."
Wife: "But I rule the rooster."

Did you hear about the conceited rooster?
He stood on top of a roof, whether vane or not.

Saint Bernard

Did you hear about the kind old lady who had the face of a saint?

Unfortunately, it was a Saint Bernard.

Sardine

What happened to the sardine factory employees who didn't show up for work?

They got canned.

Where is the best place to set up a sardine processing plant?

The Cannery Islands.

Seagull

What do you call musical birds flying in formation over the ocean?

Chorus gulls.

If a seagull flies over the sea, what flies over the bay?

A bagel.

Two men were walking along the beach when a seagull deposited a load right smack in one guy's eye.

The other fellow thoughtfully offered, "Let me get some toilet paper."

"Forget it," the victim replied. "It's probably a mile away by now."

Seahorse

Why did the sportsman buy a seahorse?

He wanted to play water polo.

Seal

Did you hear about the guy who went on a raw fish diet?

He didn't lose much weight, but he can balance a ball on his nose and bark like a seal.

Seeing-Eye Dog

In the early 1700s, the captain of a Spanish pirate ship was very proud of his mongrel pet for its ability to bark once for "si" and twice for "no." After being captured by a British commander, the dog was taught the same trick in English. He thereby became the world's first "si" and "aye" dog.

Setter

Did you hear about the man who used his dog as a tea tray?

Mind you, the dog was often upset.

Shark

Two sharks were swimming near the shore when one suddenly asked, "What was that two-legged thing that just came into the water?"

"I don't know," replied the other. "I'll bite."

What do you call those rubber bumpers on yachts?
Shark absorbers.

Shark carpenters are hammerheads.

Sheep

When they are trying to fall asleep, do sheep count people?

How many sheep does it take to make a sweater?
It depends on how well they can knit.

How were the lambs launched into space?
In a rocket sheep. They became the herd shot round the world.

What is a sheep's favorite newspaper?
The Wool Street Journal.

Why did the couple put sheep rugs throughout their new home?
They wanted wool-to-wool carpeting.

Sheepdog

Did you hear about the two shaggy sheepdogs that were madly in love?

One moonlit night, the male was feeling romantic and gushed, "My matchless Melissa, I daresay that I cannot live another day without you. Ah, you are Melissa, aren't you?"

Skunk

How much is a skunk worth?
One scent.

How do you stop a skunk from smelling?
Hold its nose.

What did the skunk say when the wind turned?
"It all comes back to me, now."

What did one skunk say to another when they were cornered outside a church?
"Let us spray."

Slug

How is the snail housing market?
A bit sluggish.

Snail

As the snail said to the turtle, "What's the rush?"

Patient: "Doctor, doctor! I feel like I'm a snail."

Doctor: "Just try to come out of your shell."

What do escargots use to paint their toes?
Snail polish.

Snake

When was the blame game first played?
*Adam blamed Eve, and Eve blamed the serpent.
And the serpent didn't have a leg to stand on.*

Boy No. 1: "I saw a six-foot snake."
Boy No. 2: "I didn't think snakes had feet."

What is the name of the queen's pet snake?
Hiss Majesty.

Did you hear about the nearsighted hiker?
He picked up a snake to kill a stick.

Oh well. When it comes to snake jokes, you can't venom all.

Sow

One female pig said to another, "Sow's things?"
The second pig answered, "Sow sow."

Spider

Did you hear about the spider that asked to test drive a car?
> *He just wanted to take it for a spin.*

What did Miss Muffet say when the spider asked her for a date?
> *"Ha! No whey!"*

Squirrel

As one squirrel said to her friend, "I'd go out on a limb for you."

Did you hear about the squirrels that developed an assembly-line nut-gathering process?
> *They were autumn-mated. (And they were able to squirrel away many nuts at a time.)*

Steer

> *Cautious rider to her reckless dear:*
> *"Let's have less bull and lots more steer."*

Stork

A stork is a baby bird.

Who delivers baby whales?
> *A stork with a bad back.*

Swine

Did you hear about the squealing physicist?
> *His name was Albert Einswine.*

Tapir

Did you hear about the overweight jungle animal with a long snout?

It decided to tapir off its eating.

Termite

Young termites are babes in the wood.

Old termites never die. They just live happily ever rafter.

Tick

What crazy arachnids live on the moon?
Lunatics.

Man: "Doctor, doctor! What should I do with my watchdog that has ticks?"
Vet: "Don't wind him."

Tiger

Man No. 1: "Would you rather have a lion attack you or a tiger?"
Man No. 2: "I'd rather it attacked the tiger."

What are the most popular flowers in a zoo?
The dandelion and the tiger lily.

Toad

What children's song did country singer Willie Nelson write about riding on a giant frog?
"On the Toad Again."

What do you call Native American amphibians that sit one on top of another?
A toadem pole.

Or, as the frustrated father frog said to his daughter, "If I've toad you once, I've toad you a thousand times . . ."

Tuna

Did you hear about the tuna who went to Hollywood?
It wanted to be a starfish.

Turkey

Why did they let the turkey join the band?
Because it had the drumsticks.

Is turkey soup good for your health?
Not if you're the turkey.

Why did the turkey cross the road?
To show he wasn't chicken.

What happened when the turkey got into a fight?
He got the stuffing knocked out of him.

How are a turkey, a donkey, and a monkey the same?
They all have keys.

Turtle

TV interviewer: "How's business?"
Turtle salesman: "Slow."

Did you hear about the nearsighted turtle?
He fell in love with an army helmet.

Unicorn

Why is a lisping unicorn always female?
Because the unicorn is a myth.

Vampire

Why are vampires sad?
Because they love in vein.

Where does Count Dracula usually eat his lunch?
At the casketeria.

Why did the vampire go into a fast-food restaurant?
For a quick bite.

Did you hear about the vampire who was fired as night watchman at a blood bank?

They caught him drinking on the job.

How many vampires does it take to change a light bulb?

None. Vampires prefer the dark.

What's the difference between an optimist and a vampire killer?

One counts his blessings, and the other blesses his counts.

How do you say good-bye to a vampire?

"So long, sucker!"

Vulture

Did you hear about the guy who does bird imitations?

He eats like a vulture.

Weevil

What is the menace of the bug world?
The weevil empire.

When he found bugs feasting on an embalmed body, the Egyptian undertaker said, "Mummy is the loot of all weevil."

Werewolf

Where does a werewolf live?
In a werehouse.

Whale

A bunch of whales at a party had a people of a time.

What's the favorite TV show of aquarium employees?
Whale of Fortune.

Did you hear about the nearsighted whale that fell in love with a submarine?
Every time the boat fired a torpedo, the proud whale handed out cigars.

Or, as one whale complained to another, "Why are you always spouting off?"

Wolf

What is a wolf's favorite song?
"Howl, Howl, the Gang's All Here!"

Woodpecker

Did you hear about the unpopular woodpecker?
He was boring company.

What is green and pecks on trees?
Woody Woodpickle.

Worm

Did you hear about the worm that joined the marines?
It wanted to be in the apple corps.

Apple No. 1: "What's the matter? What's eating you?"
Apple No. 2: "Worms."

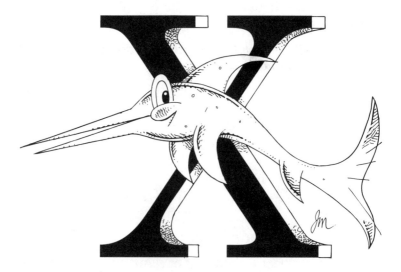

Xiphiidae

There's a little-known animal that begins with the letter X. It's actually a Greek swordfish, spelled *x-i-p-h-i-i-d-a-e*, and it's pronounced *"ziff-EYE-ih-dee."* With that in mind, what did the Greek swordfish sing when it was feeling happy?

"Zip-a-dee doo-dah, xiphiidae-ay."

Yak

There once was a man in Tibet
Who worked in the hills as a vet.
He treated the backs
Of overworked yaks;
How low (or how high) can one get?

What ox will never be seen?
A yak in a kayak.

Zebra

Did you hear about the zebra in a hurricane?
He had to glue on his stripes.

What has stars and stripes?
A movie about a zebra.

Zebu

What did the Asian ox say to his friends?
"Zebu all later."

PART 2
EVEN MORE
ANIMAL JOKES

50 Rhyming Animals

Have you ever seen an antelope grope, an asp grasp, a bee flee, a boar soar, a bull pull, cattle battle, a clam jam, a cod nod, a coot shoot, a crane train, a crocodile smile, a deer sneer, a doe row, a drake rake, an eel peel, a ewe queue, a finch pinch, a fish wish, a foal roll, a frog blog, a giraffe laugh, a gnu chew, a grackle cackle, a hawk gawk, a hog jog, a hound bound, a kangaroo woo, a lion cryin', a manatee ban a tea, a mole bowl, a mule duel, a nag brag, a parakeet eat, a poodle doodle, a rabbit grab it, a rat chat, a roach coach, a seal steal, a sheep leap, a shrimp limp, a snail wail, a snake shake, a sow bow, a squid bid, a steer veer, a swine whine, a tick pick, a trout spout, a turtle hurtle, and a worm squirm?

15 Fly-in-the-Soup Jokes

Customer: "Waiter, there's a fly in my soup."
Waiter: "Well, you asked that your soup have a little body."

Customer: "Waiter, there's a fly in my soup."
Waiter: "What did you expect for $3, clams?"

Customer: "Waiter, there's a fly in my soup."
Waiter: "So? How much can it eat?"

Customer: "Waiter, there's a fly in my soup."
Waiter: "Don't worry. The spider will eat it before you do."

Customer: "Waiter, there's a fly in my soup."
Waiter: "Shhh! All the other customers will want one."

Customer: "Waiter, there's a bee in my soup."
Waiter: "It's alphabet soup, sir."

Customer: "Waiter, there's a fly in my alphabet soup."
Waiter: "That's not a fly. That's a spelling bee."

Customer: "Waiter, there's a fly in my soup."
Waiter: "Ask it if it wants to see a menu."

Customer: "Waiter, there's a fly in my soup."
Waiter: "That's strange. I thought the cook had used all of them in the raisin bread."

Customer: "Waiter, there's a fly in my soup."
Waiter: "I'm sorry. I didn't realize you were a vegetarian."

Customer: "What's this fly doing in my soup?"
Waiter: "The backstroke, I believe."

Customer: "Waiter, what's this fly doing in my ice cream?"
Waiter: "It's downhill skiing, I believe."

Customer: "Waiter, there are three flies in my soup."
Waiter: "Wow, the chef must really like you."

A frog walked into a restaurant and ordered a meal and then asked the waiter, "Why isn't there a fly in my soup?"

A customer accidentally spilled soup on his lap and cried out, "Waiter, there's soup in my fly!"

10 Classroom Classics

Teacher: "Use *gladiator* in a sentence."
Student: "The farmer's hen stopped laying eggs, so he was gladiator."

Teacher: "Where does mohair come from?"
Student: "From a goat named Moe."

Teacher: "What is the opposite of *sorrow*?"
Student: "*Joy.*"
Teacher: "That's right. Now what's the opposite of *misery*?"
Student: "*Happiness.*"
Teacher: "Right again. Now what's the opposite of *woe*?"
Student: "*Giddy up.*"

Teacher: "What is the equator?"
Student: "It's a menagerie lion running around the middle of the earth."

Teacher: "Please spell *mouse.*"
Student: "M–O–U–S."
Teacher: "But what's at the end of it?"
Student: "A tail."

Teacher: "What is pigskin used for?"
Student: "It's for holding pigs together."

Teacher (before Thanksgiving): "What are you thankful for?"
Student: "I'm thankful that I'm not a turkey."

Teacher: "What is a vegetarian?"
Student: "It's a horse doctor."
Teacher: "No. You're thinking of a veterinarian."
Student: "I thought a veterinarian was a former member of the armed forces."

Teacher: "Eskimos eat whale meat and blubber."

Student: "I'd blubber, too, if all I had to eat was whale meat."

Teacher: "If the statue of George Washington in front of City Hall could speak, what do you think he would say today?"

Student: "He'd say, 'I hate pigeons.'"

15 Animal Crossings

What do you get when you cross two punsters with a hen?

Two comedians who lay eggs with a lot of bad yolks.

In these days of genetic miracles, you never can tell what you'll end up with when you combine one animal with another animal.

What do you get when you cross . . .

. . . a flea with a rabbit?

A bugs bunny.

. . . Snoopy with the American bird?

A bald beagle.

. . . an octopus with a dragon?

An octagon.

. . . a cow with a mule?

Milk with a real kick to it.

. . . a pointer with a setter?

A poinsettia.

. . . a lion with a parrot?

We don't know what it is, but when it talks, you better listen!

. . . a rabbit with a frog?

A bunny ribbit.

. . . a kangaroo with a newborn snake?

A bouncing baby boa.

. . . a wolf with a rooster?

An animal that howls when the sun rises and goes cock-a-doodle-doo at night.

. . . a skunk with a deer?

A dirty look from the deer.

. . . a skunk with an owl?

An animal that smells awful but doesn't give a hoot.

. . . a giraffe with a swordfish?

The wildest looking tree surgeon you ever saw.

. . . a giraffe with a rooster?

An animal that wakes you up on the top floor.

. . . a dog with a kangaroo?

A pooch with a pouch.

. . . a chilipepper, a shovel, and a poodle?

A hot diggity dog.

10 Animal Contrasts

What's the difference between a healthy rabbit and the authors of this book?

> *One is a fit bunny, and the others are a bit funny.*

And what's the difference between . . .

. . . a butcher and a night owl?

> *One weighs a steak, and the other stays awake.*

. . . a fish and a piano?

> *You can't tuna fish.*

. . . a tiger and a lion?

> *The tiger has the mane part missing.*

. . . a pigeon and a poor farmer?

> *The pigeon can still make a deposit on a new barn.*

. . . an American buffalo and an Australian bison?

> *You can't wash your hands in a buffalo.*

. . . cash your mom lent you and the price of a skunk?

> *One is money owed her, and the other is odor money.*

. . . a baby frog and the month's rent?

> *One is a tadpole, and the other is a pad toll.*

. . . a jumping magician and a crying gecko?

> *One is a leaping wizard, and the other is a weeping lizard.*

. . . a mangy hyena and a dead stinging insect?

> *One is a seedy beast, and the other is a bee deceased.*

. . bird flu and swine flu?

> *For bird flu you need tweetment. For swine flu you need an oinkment.*

30 Daffynitions

Somebody once defined *vitamin* as "what you do when stray cats come to your home." These "daffynitions" take a fresh approach to the sounds of familiar words, and some of the daffiest can be found in the animal kingdom:

Alarms: What an octopus is.

Apex: A gorilla's old girlfriend.

Ascent: What a hunting dog follows.

Asleep: A donkey's jump.

Avoidable: What a smart matador does.

Bambino: A negative response from a mother deer.

Beehive: What an Australian schoolteacher tells an unruly child.

Billy club: A night spot for goats.

Bookworm: A person who would rather read than eat, or a worm that would rather eat than read.

Caterpillar: A soft scratching post for a cat.

Cheetah: A cat that peeks at another cat's test.

Chimpanzee: A monkey's favorite flower.

Derange: Where de deer and de antelope play.

Donkey: The most difficult key to turn.

Flypaper: An airmail letter.

Guacamole: An animal that tunnels through avocado fields.

Hillbilly: A goat living at a high altitude.

Hogwash: A place for cleaning pigs.

Information: How geese fly.

Mosquito: An insect that bites the hand that feeds it.

Mushroom: A place where Eskimos train their sled dogs.

Ostracize: A workout for large birds.

Panther: A big cat that panths.

Posse: A cat in the Wild West.

Propaganda: A politically correct male goose.

Render: An animal that pulls Santa's sleigh.

Sherbet: A horse that never loses a race.

Steel wool: Rob a sheep farm.

Toad: Dragged cousin of a frog.

Touchdown: Feel goose feathers.

10 Knock-Knock Jokes

Knock, knock. *Who's there?* Canoe. *Canoe who?* Canoe guess the punch lines to these knock-knock jokes about animals?

Knock, knock.
Who's there?
Anna.
Anna who?
Anna partridge in a pear tree.

Knock, knock.
Who's there?
Centipede.
Centipede who?
Centipede on the Christmas tree.

Knock, knock.
Who's there?
Goat.
Goat who?
Goat to your room!

Knock, knock.
Who's there?
Lionel.
Lionel who?
Lionel roar if it's not fed.

Knock, knock.
Who's there?
Noel.
Noel who?
No elephant is going to stick his trunk in my business.

Knock, knock.
Who's there?
Oily.
Oily who?
The oily bird catches the worm.

Knock, knock.
Who's there?
Pooch.
Pooch who?
Pooch your arms around me.

Knock, knock.
Who's there?
Possum.
Possum who?
Possum potatoes, please.

Knock, knock.
Who's there?
Rude and interrupting cow.
Rude and inte—
Moo!

Knock, knock.
Who's there?
Who.
Who who?
An owl like you.

Knock, knock. *Who's there?* Orange. *Orange who?* Now orange you glad that you read all these knock-knock jokes?

10 Worst Animal Maladies

- a hippopotamus with chapped lips
- a cow that's lactose intolerant
- a bear with insomnia
- a ram with a headache
- an octopus with underarm odor
- a seasick whale
- a shark with a toothache
- a yak with dandruff
- a bloodhound with a stuffy nose
- a bee with an allergy to flowers

15 Animal Jokes in Black and White

The original joke goes like this: What's black and white and red all over? And the answer is a newspaper (because it's printed in black on white paper and is *read* all over).

That riddle has become so popular that over the years it has become a whole series of animal jokes:

What's black and white and red all over?
> *A blushing zebra.*

What's black and white and red all over?
> *A sunburned penguin.*

What's black and white and red all over?
> *A skunk with diaper rash.*

What's black and white and red all over?
> *A Dalmatian with measles.*

What's black and white and red all over?
> *A skunk that spilled catsup on itself.*

Why do zebras have black and white stripes?
> *So they can referee football games.*

What's black and white and blue all over?
> *A panda in a refrigerator.*

What's black and white and blue all over?
> *An ostrich holding its breath.*

What's black and white and has eight wheels?
> *A penguin on roller skates.*

What's black and white and has four wheels?
> *A zebra. We lied about the wheels.*

What's black and white and green and black and white?
Two Dalmatians fighting over a pickle.

What's black and white and green and yellow and purple
and black and blue?
An ostrich and a pheasant in a fistfight.

What's black and white and black and white?
A penguin dressed up in a nun's habit.

What's black and white and black and white and black
and white and black and white?
A skunk caught in a revolving door.

What's black and white and black and white and black
and white and black and white and black and white and
black and white and black and white and black and white
and black and white and black and white and black and
white and black and white and black and white and black
and white and black and white and black and white and
black and white and black and white and black and white
and black and white and black and white and black and
white and black and white and black and white and black
and white and black and white and black and white and
black and white and black and white and black and white
and black and white and black and white and black and\
white and black and white and black and white and black
and white and black and white and black and white and
black and white and black and white and black and white
and black and white and black and white and black and
white and black and white and black and white and black
and white and black and white and black and white and
black and white and black and white and black and white
and black and white and black and white and black and
white and black and white and black and white and black

and white and black and white and black and white and
black and white and black and white and black and white
and black and white and black and white and black and
white and black and white and black and white and black
and white and black and white and black and white and
black and white and black and white and black and white
and black and white and black and white and black and
white and black and white and black and white and black
and white and black and white and black and white and
black and white and black and white and black and white
and black and white and black and white and black and
white and black and white and black and white and black
and white and black and white and black and white and
black and white and black and white and black and white
and black and white and black and white and black and
white and black and white and black and white?

The answer is *101 Dalmatians.*

35 Animal Anagrams

An anagram is a rearrangement of all the letters in a word or group of words to form another word or group of words. Thus, *parrot* and *raptor* are anagrams of each other because they both contain the same letters but each in a different order.

In the examples that follow, all the letters in each animal's name form all the letters in the word or words that come before or after that name:

Have you ever seen a hare hear, rhea hear, wasp swap, wolf flow, snake sneak, pinto point, trout tutor, egret greet, mite emit, lobster bolster, sole lose, tern rent, steer reset, mare ream, foal loaf, civet evict, manatee emanate, butterfly flutter by, pets step, cats cast, a meerkat e-market, and emus muse?

And have you ever seen slow owls, star rats, snug gnus, sobbing gibbons, snorted rodents, unshod hounds, spooled poodles, spider prides, noiseless lionesses, snug pine penguins, pie song pigeons, and ten skit kittens in a cat act?

10 Cat Palindromes

A palindrome is a word, like *level*; a compound, like *senile felines*; or a sentence, like the examples that follow, that communicates the same message both forwards and backwards. Have fun reading each statement and then in reverse.

STACK CATS.

TACKLE ELK CAT.

WOE ME: "MEOW!"

WAS IT A CAT I SAW?

PURR. IT'S A STIRRUP.

SO, CATNIP IN TACOS?

WE MOOCH, COO, MEW.

NO, SIT! CAT ACT IS ON.

SENILE FEMALES, RODNEY AWAY, ENDORSE LAME FELINES.

ARE WE NOT DRAWN ONWARD, TACO CAT, DRAWN ONWARD TO NEW ERA?

Collect the Whole Series!

IN STORES NOW!